A Guide Dog Named Arby

Story by Karrie Roberts
Illustrated by Billy Leavenworth

REDEMPTION
PRESS

Published by Redemption Press, PO Box 427, Enumclaw, WA 98022

Toll Free (844) 2REDEEM (273-3336)

Redemption Press is honored to present this title in partnership with the author. The views expressed or implied in this work are those of the author. Redemption Press provides our imprint seal representing design excellence, creative content, and high quality production.

Cover design by Amber Weigand-Buckley.

ISBN 13: 978-1-68314-136-5 (Print)

978-1-68314-199-0 ePub

978-1-68314-200-3 Mobi

Library of Congress Catalog Card Number: 2016960828

We would like to acknowledge the following people for their support and encouragement in the pre-purchase of "A Guide Dog Named Arby". There were many more that are not listed and we want to thank and acknowledge everyone who has been a part of this journey! We pray that this book will continue to educate, motivate, and inspire, your family and your friends for years to come!

Aaron & Janaye Kemp, Liam & Lillie

Aaron & Melody Woodall

Andrea Michaels of Edward Jones

Bill & Deborah Littler

Bill & Laura Hetrick on behalf of Paws with Promise Puppy Raisers

Billy & Elaine Leavenworth, (our amazing illustrator and his lovely wife!)

Bruce and Josh Hudson of Hudson's Portrait Design

Burke & Jen Bordner on behalf of Lucy, Mia, Charlie, & Sam

Carl & Jeanette Bessent on behalf of Guide Dog Nerice, and Evi & Hazel

Carolyn Rasmussen on behalf of Richard Rogers

Catherine Colebank on behalf of Grayson

Clark Roberts on behalf of my amazing guide dogs Missy, Toddy, Lacey, Arbuckle (Arby) and Aurelia

Cliff & Nicki Anderson

Dave Young on behalf of Chloe, Callie, & Carmen

Dawn Weaver

Deb Ferguson on behalf of John C. Ostlund

Debbie Bartell

Desiree' Burgess of Harts & Pearls, on behalf of Hartley

Eva Jahan on behalf of Zahra Crawford

Gary & Kathy Taylor, Alexis, Abbie, Austin and Cody

Irene Dunkerton on behalf of William Crow

Jacob & Anne-Elise Anderson

Jared & Rachael Lynn, Lina & Cora

Jerry & Kristi Lynn on behalf of Lina, Cora, Liam & Lillie

Jim Humphries

John & Victoria Panaccione on behalf of OC Coastal Puppy Club

Kathie DeBarr

Kay Kinssies on behalf of Selah & Noll Kelly

Kelly Berge

Kelly Nordstrom on behalf of Jaffrey & Everett Westcott

Larry & Alice Shultz

Mark & Sarah Hamilton on behalf of Elizabeth, Cole and Bear

Mark Haight of Haight Carpet and Interiors

Michelle Wilkenson

Nick Jones & Tina Xidias-Jones of BooBoo Barkery & Boutique on behalf of Kiwi & Charlie

Omar Rivas

Rachel Bradshaw on behalf of Levi & Axel Schneider

Rachel Hile on behalf of Luke, Clara & Caleb

Rachel Lynn

Ron & Karen Moore

Steve & Betty Bordner on behalf of Reese, Kendall, Brooklyn, and Duke

Steve & Rachel Benedict on behalf of Grace, Andy & Cooper

Susan Alkema in honor of Billy Leavenworth

Susan Mangis on behalf of guide dog Jenna

Tamara Hill on behalf of Britni, Fender and Gibson

Tammy Wallace on behalf of Shannon and service dog Levi

Thomas & Stacy Wolter on behalf of Zechariah, Elijah, & Siri

Tianxiu Dai

Traci Burgess of Stella & Dot

Dedication:

To my Lord and Savior who gave me the gift of words. To my husband Clark—you inspire me daily to dream. To Jacob & Rebekah who I write for and who never stopped believing in me and encouraged me to publish my children's stories, always remember Philippians 4:13 "The 10 Finger Prayer!"

Hi, my name is Arby.

I'm not your normal pet.

I am called a guide dog.

Do you know what I do?

Can you guess?

I was born in California.

In the place that I called home,

Guide Dogs for the Blind,

As a puppy I did roam.

I have eight brothers and sisters.

Our names begin with "A."

When we were young

We had fun running and barking,

And all we did was eat,

Sleep,

And PLAY!

When I was eight weeks old,

I got in my crate and packed it

With my toys,

My blanket,

And my little green jacket.

Then I rode in a truck to my puppy raiser.

I was so excited to greet them,

I wiggled and I waggled,

I couldn't wait to meet them.

My puppy raiser had the job
Of taking me out on the town,
And helping me
get used to ...
Sights, smells,
and sounds.

We went on field trips,
Because learning to behave was the key.
Museums, libraries, ferries, and buses—
So much for me to see!

When we went for burgers and ice cream
I was learning to behave on cue.
So when I heard the command, "Leave it,"
I knew just what to do!

My jacket was my ticket

Everywhere we would go.

"Guide Puppy in Training" was stitched on it,

So everyone would know.

At times my friends would join us.

They would bring their puppy raisers, too.

People loved to stop and ask,

"What is it that you do?"

I'm a special kind of dog,

Born to do a special task,

From a place called Guide Dogs for the Blind.

I'm so glad you asked!

As I grew into a bigger dog,

I left my puppy raiser and

went away to school.

I traded my jacket for a harness,

And began to learn the rules.

The more I learned the more I knew

How special my job was to be.

I was matched with a person who was blind,

A person who could not see.

This person took ahold
Of my harness handle,
Gave me the command "forward,"
And I began to lead.

Both of us were learning
While we were in school.
You see, I am now a working guide dog,
And it's important to follow the rules!

I bet that you like food ... so do I!

But while I am working I must be safe,

So never ever feed me

Or put food near my face.

Another rule that's important,

Especially when the weather is hotter,

Is no matter how I look at you

Never, ever give me water.

22

Then there's the rule about my harness,

Which is the handle on my back.

You must not hold on to it EVER!

Only my partner should do that.

The last and most important rule

Is to help keep me on my task.

Never reach out and pet me.

You must always remember to ASK.

If you cannot remember these rules,

Find an adult to ask.

Because keeping all these rules

Will help me with my task

Of getting my person
From place to place,
And helping to keep both of us
Happy, healthy, and safe.

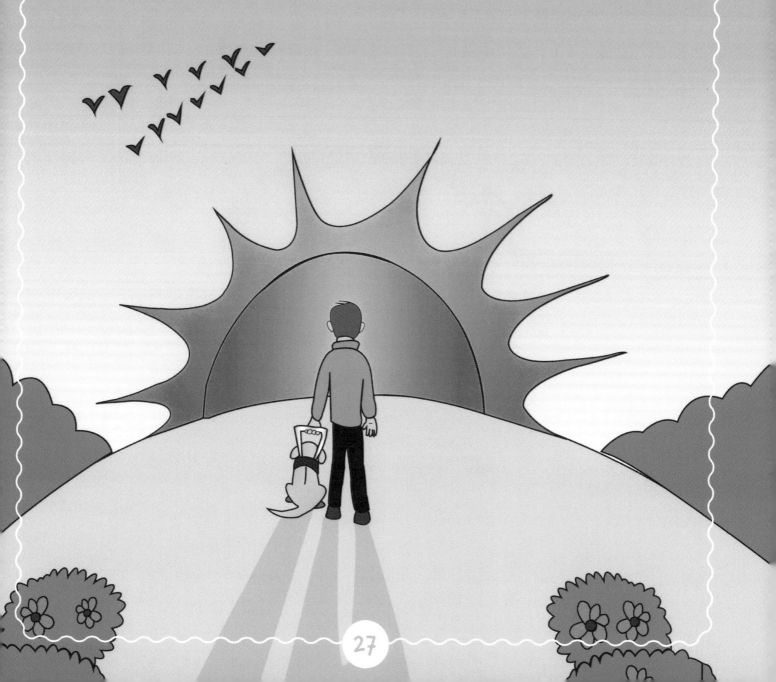

I hope you were listening

To my story of what I do.

Now it's time to ask some questions—

Questions just for you!

1. What is the dog's name in the story? Arby

2. Where was he born? california

3. What color is his jacket? green

4. What does the jacket say? guide puppy in training

5. Who took Arby on field trips?

6. What job does a guide dog do?

7. Who does a guide dog help?

8. What Character Trait does Arby teach you?

9. What do you call the item on his back?

10. What are the 4 rules to remember?

I'm a Guide Dog

Hi, I'm Arby—yes, that's me

I help a person who cannot see.

Remember, I'm a special dog

Born to do a special job.

I'm a guide dog, yes, it's true.

Here are rules just for you.

Please don't pet me, always ask.

This will keep me on my task.

Never feed me your goldfish,

Or put water in my dish.

About the harness on my back,

Only my partner touches that.

Yep, I'm Arby—yes, that's me.

I help a person who cannot see.

Now you know I'm a special dog,

Born to do a special job.

I'm a guide dog, yes, that's true.

And now you know what I can do.

Lyrics by Karrie Roberts
2015

Teachable Moments:

Take time to talk to your child or children about what
they thought of the story. What did they learn?
What did they find interesting or funny?
What questions do they have?
What character traits did they find in this story?
Who showed the character traits, and how
did they demonstrate them?
How can you and your child show
these character traits?

Share with your friends and family
what you learned.

Look for these character traits in A Guide Dog Named Arby.

Character Trait RESPONSIBILITY

How was Arby showing this trait?

How can you show this trait?

Character Trait OBEDIENCE

How was Arby showing this trait?

How can you show this trait?

Character Trait LOYALTY

How was Arby showing this trait?

How can you show this trait?

Character Trait GENEROSITY

How was Arby showing this trait?

How can you show this trait?

Character Trait TRUST

How was Arby showing this trait?

How can you show this trait?

Other Character Traits:

SELF CONTROL, KNOWLEDGE, PATIENCE, & LOVE

About Arby

Arbuckle is a quirky purebred yellow Labrador who was born on December 11, 2006, at the Guide Dogs For the Blind campus in San Rafael, California. At the age of eight weeks old he met the Clark family in Spokane Washington. The Clarks would be Arbuckle's puppy raising family for almost two years. After being fully trained Arbuckle (Arby) would be partnered with Clark Roberts on September 06, 2008 and would guide for Clark for the next 7 years.

During this time Arby accompanied and led Clark on many adventures which included multiple speaking engagements delivering a message of hope and encouragement to people young and old. Arby also accompanied Clark to fun events like skydiving at Sky Dive Snohomish, the Museum of Flight in Seattle Washington and other fun memorable activities. Arby was always happy to share in scritches and belly rubs while he was traveling.

Arby retired from guiding on September 13, 2015 and now resides with Jacob and Anne-Elise Anderson in Bellevue, Washington where he enjoys sleeping, playing and receiving multiple belly rubs. Arby will continue to join us (as long as he is able) in public appearances and book signings where he will provide all humans with his pawdograph.

Contact Information

To order additional copies of this book, please visit
www.redemption-press.com.
Also available on Amazon.com and BarnesandNoble.com
Or by calling toll free 1-844-2REDEEM.

CPSIA information can be obtained at www.ICGtesting.com
Printed in the USA
BVIW12n0608290817
493081BV00003B/3